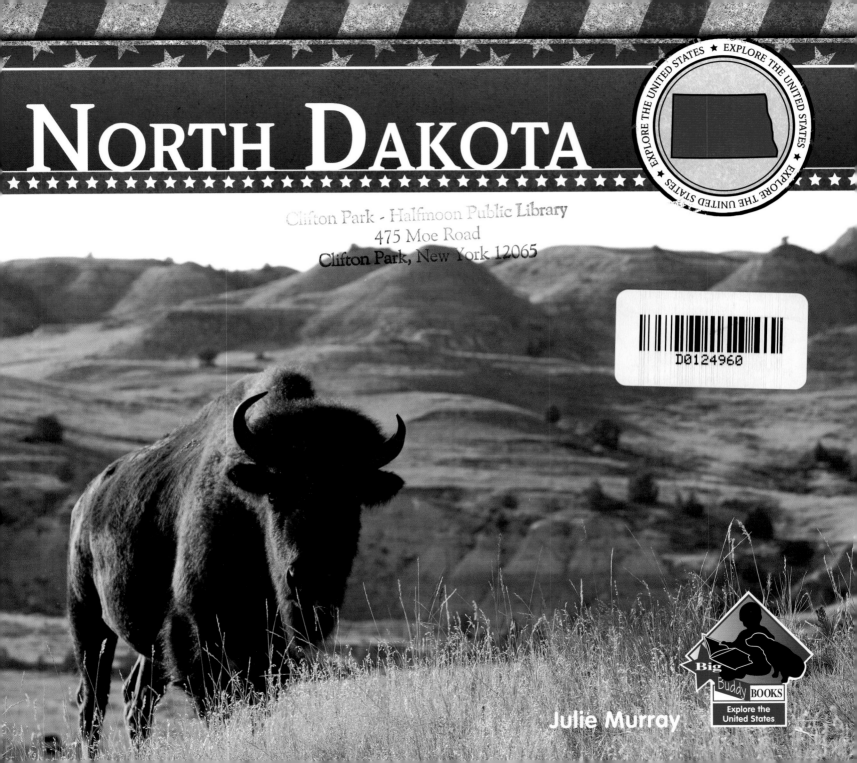

NORTH DAKOTA

EXPLORE THE UNITED STATES ★ EXPLORE THE UNITED STATES ★ EXPLORE THE UNITED STATES ★ EXPLORE THE UNITED STATES

D0124960

Julie Murray

Big Buddy BOOKS
Explore the United States

VISIT US AT
www.abdopublishing.com

Published by ABDO Publishing Company, PO Box 398166, Minneapolis, MN 55439.

Printed in the United States of America, North Mankato, Minnesota.
052012
092012

♻ PRINTED ON RECYCLED PAPER

Coordinating Series Editor: Rochelle Baltzer
Editor: Sarah Tieck
Contributing Editors: Megan M. Gunderson, BreAnn Rumsch, Marcia Zappa
Graphic Design: Adam Craven
Cover Photograph: *iStockphoto*: ©iStockphoto.com/ericfoltz.
Interior Photographs/Illustrations: *Alamy*: Andre Jenny (p. 26), Don Smetzer (p. 27); *AP Photo*: North Wind Picture
    Archives via AP Images (p. 13), Matty Zimmerman (p. 25); *Getty Images*: Elsa (p. 27), MPI (p. 23); *Glow
    Images*: Bill Bachmann (p. 11), Barrett & MacKay (p. 27), © Tom Bean/CORBIS (p. 17), Richard Cummins
    (p. 9); *iStockphoto*: ©iStockphoto.com/JeffGoulden (p. 26), ©iStockphoto.com/jhayes44 (p. 5),
    ©iStockphoto.com/Joesboy (p. 29), ©iStockphoto.com/outtakes (p. 30), ©iStockphoto.com/KeithSzafranski
    (p. 19), ©iStockphoto.com/ThereseMcK (p. 30); *Shutterstock*: Philip Lange (p. 30), oksana2010 (p. 30),
    Wildnerdpix (p. 21).

All population figures taken from the 2010 US census.

Library of Congress Cataloging-in-Publication Data

Murray, Julie, 1969-
  North Dakota / Julie Murray.
     p. cm. -- (Explore the United States)
  ISBN 978-1-61783-372-4
  1. North Dakota--Juvenile literature. I. Title.
  F636.3.M87 2012
  978.4--dc23
                                        2012013126

6615

NORTH DAKOTA

Contents

ONE NATION

The United States is a **diverse** country. It has farmland, cities, coasts, and mountains. Its people come from many different backgrounds. And, its history covers more than 200 years.

Today the country includes 50 states. North Dakota is one of these states. Let's learn more about this state and its story!

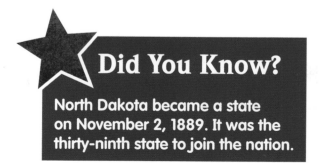

Did You Know?

North Dakota became a state on November 2, 1889. It was the thirty-ninth state to join the nation.

North Dakota's Badlands are known for unusual rock shapes.

NORTH DAKOTA UP CLOSE

The United States has four main **regions**. North Dakota is in the Midwest.

North Dakota has three states on its borders. Minnesota is east, South Dakota is south, and Montana is west. The country of Canada is north.

North Dakota has a total area of 70,698 square miles (183,107 sq km). It has the third-smallest population in the country. About 700,000 people live there.

Did You Know?

Washington DC is the US capital city. Puerto Rico is a US commonwealth. This means it is governed by its own people.

REGIONS OF THE UNITED STATES

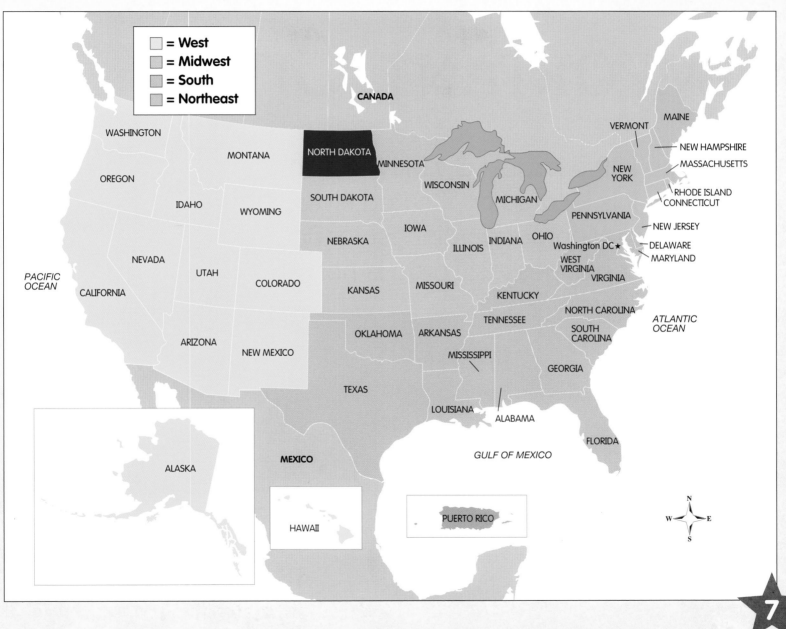

= West
= Midwest
= South
= Northeast

CANADA

WASHINGTON
MONTANA
NORTH DAKOTA
MINNESOTA
VERMONT
MAINE
NEW HAMPSHIRE
MASSACHUSETTS
OREGON
IDAHO
WYOMING
SOUTH DAKOTA
WISCONSIN
MICHIGAN
NEW YORK
RHODE ISLAND
CONNECTICUT
NEVADA
UTAH
COLORADO
NEBRASKA
IOWA
ILLINOIS
INDIANA
OHIO
PENNSYLVANIA
NEW JERSEY
Washington DC★
DELAWARE
MARYLAND
WEST VIRGINIA
VIRGINIA
PACIFIC OCEAN
CALIFORNIA
KANSAS
MISSOURI
KENTUCKY
NORTH CAROLINA
ATLANTIC OCEAN
ARIZONA
NEW MEXICO
OKLAHOMA
ARKANSAS
TENNESSEE
SOUTH CAROLINA
MISSISSIPPI
GEORGIA
TEXAS
LOUISIANA
ALABAMA
FLORIDA
GULF OF MEXICO
MEXICO
ALASKA
HAWAII
PUERTO RICO

N
W E
S

IMPORTANT CITIES

Fargo is the largest city in North Dakota. It has 105,549 people. It is located on the Red River of the North. Fargo is close to Moorhead, Minnesota. Both cities have shops and other businesses. Fargo is home to North Dakota State University.

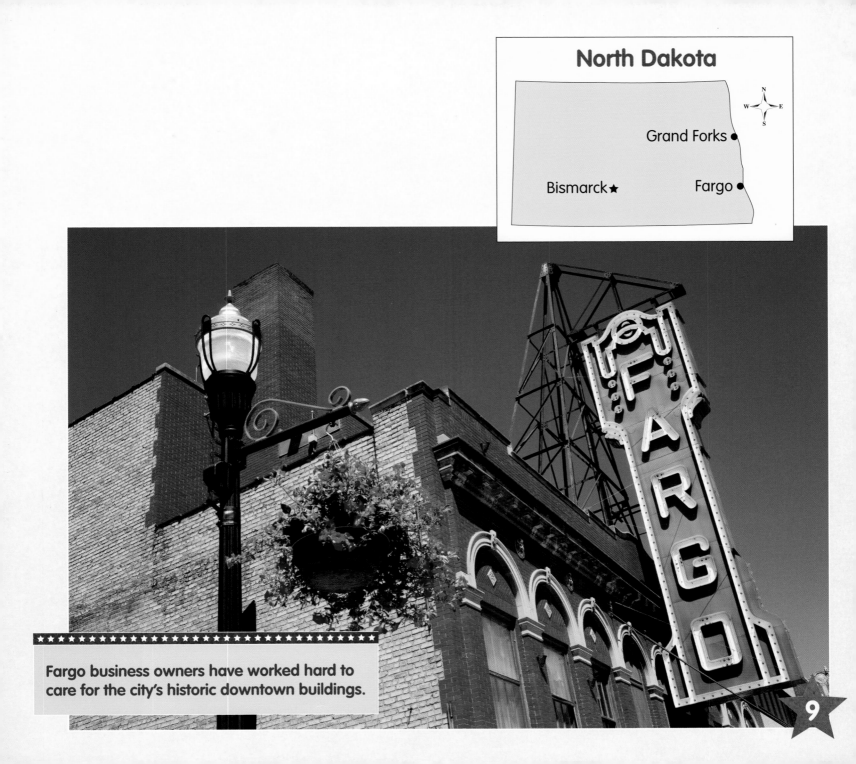

North Dakota

Grand Forks ●

Bismarck ★

Fargo ●

Fargo business owners have worked hard to care for the city's historic downtown buildings.

9

Bismarck is North Dakota's **capital**. It is also the state's second-largest city. It has 61,272 people. Visitors come to the city to spend time at nearby Fort Abraham Lincoln State Park.

Grand Forks is the third-largest city in the state. It is home to 52,838 people. The University of North Dakota is located there.

The North Dakota State Capitol was completed in 1934.

North Dakota in History

North Dakota's history includes Native Americans and settlers. Native Americans were the first to live in what is now North Dakota. Tribes built homes, hunted, and grew crops in the area.

In 1682, French explorers claimed the land. In 1803, President Thomas Jefferson bought land from France. Much of present-day North Dakota was part of this land. Over time, many settlers came. North Dakota became a state in 1889.

Did You Know?

The Mandan, Arikara, and Sioux were among the tribes that first lived in what is now North Dakota.

The Mandan built large, earth-covered homes.

13

Timeline

1803

President Thomas Jefferson bought much of present-day North Dakota as part of the **Louisiana Purchase**.

1861

Congress created the Dakota Territory.

1863

The Dakota Territory opened for **homesteading**. Over time, settlers arrived.

1800s

1804

Meriwether Lewis and William Clark explored North Dakota. They established Fort Mandan before leaving in 1805.

1889

The Dakota Territory became the states of North Dakota and South Dakota on November 2.

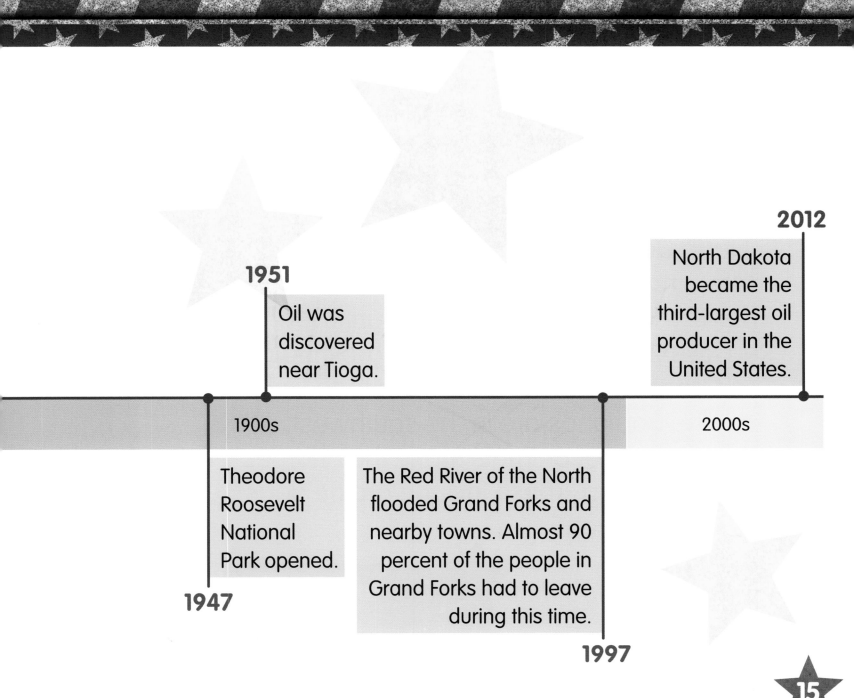

1951

Oil was discovered near Tioga.

2012

North Dakota became the third-largest oil producer in the United States.

1900s

2000s

Theodore Roosevelt National Park opened.

1947

The Red River of the North flooded Grand Forks and nearby towns. Almost 90 percent of the people in Grand Forks had to leave during this time.

1997

ACROSS THE LAND

North Dakota has flat, open land, rolling hills, rivers, and small lakes. Major rivers are the Red River of the North and the Missouri River. The Red River Valley has rich soil for growing crops. The **Great Plains** cover western North Dakota. And, the Badlands are in the southwest.

Many types of animals make their homes in North Dakota. These include prairie dogs, ducks, and bison.

Did You Know?

In July, the average temperature in North Dakota is 70°F (21°C). In January, it is 7°F (-14°C).

North Dakota's grassy lands have small lakes called potholes. Wild ducks nest in them.

Earning a Living

North Dakota has many important businesses. Some make farm machinery and foods. Many people work for banks, **insurance** companies, trucking companies, and railroads. Others have jobs in the military or helping visitors.

North Dakota has many natural **resources**. Farms produce grain and beef. And, the state's land is rich in oil.

Much oil is found in northwestern North Dakota. It is pumped from the ground.

NATURAL WONDER

The Badlands are in southwestern North Dakota. They are made up of sandstone and clay formations. The rock has bands of color that appear to change with water and light. And, water changes the shape of the rock over time.

The state's Badlands are part of Theodore Roosevelt National Park. People visit the park to camp, hike, and see the land.

Did You Know?

South Dakota also has an area called the Badlands.

Theodore Roosevelt National Park was named to honor President Theodore Roosevelt. He first visited the area in 1883.

HOMETOWN HEROES

Many famous people have lived in North Dakota. Sacagawea (sa-kuh-juh-WEE-uh) was born around 1787 near the border of present-day Idaho and Montana. She was a Shoshone Native American. When she was young, another tribe captured her and took her to North Dakota.

Sacagawea helped Meriwether Lewis and William Clark explore the United States. She and her husband joined them in North Dakota in 1804. They helped them travel through wild, unsettled lands.

Sacagawea helped the explorers talk with Native Americans they met on their journey.

Roger Maris was born in Hibbing, Minnesota, in 1934. But, he grew up in Fargo.

Maris was a famous **professional** baseball player. In 1961, he hit 61 home runs while playing for the New York Yankees. This set a record that lasted until 1998!

Maris hit a total of 275 home runs as a professional baseball player.

Tour Book

Do you want to go to North Dakota? If you visit the state, here are some places to go and things to do!

★ Visit

Learn about Native American traditions and history at one of the state's reservations. These include Turtle Mountain, Devils Lake, Fort Berthold, and Standing Rock.

★ See

Drive through North Dakota's grassy lands. Look for herds of bison and antelope!

★ Remember

Learn about the state's past. Visit the North Dakota Heritage Center in Bismarck.

★ Cheer

Watch a college hockey game! The University of North Dakota's hockey team has won seven national championships!

★ Discover

See a clock made of flowers, walk garden paths, and hear a bell tower chime. These are features of the International Peace Garden. This park borders Canada and North Dakota.

A GREAT STATE

The story of North Dakota is important to the United States. The people and places that make up this state offer something special to the country. Together with all the states, North Dakota helps make the United States great.

North Dakota is famous for its flat, open spaces.

Fast Facts

Date of Statehood:
November 2, 1889

Population (rank):
672,591
(48th most-populated state)

Total Area (rank):
70,698 square miles
(18th largest state)

Motto:
"Liberty and Union, Now and
Forever, One and Inseparable"

Nickname:
Flickertail State, Sioux State,
Peace Garden State

State Capital:
Bismarck

Flag:

Flower: Wild Prairie Rose

Postal Abbreviation:
ND

Tree: American Elm

Bird: Western Meadowlark

Important Words

capital a city where government leaders meet.

diverse made up of things that are different from each other.

Great Plains an area of dry, grassy land in North America. It includes parts of ten states.

homestead to settle on public land.

insurance a contract that promises to guard people against a loss of money if something happens to them or their property.

Louisiana Purchase land the United States purchased from France in 1803. It extended from the Mississippi River to the Rocky Mountains and from Canada through the Gulf of Mexico.

professional (pruh-FEHSH-nuhl) working for money rather than for pleasure.

region a large part of a country that is different from other parts.

resource a supply of something useful or valued.

Web Sites

To learn more about North Dakota, visit ABDO Publishing Company online. Web sites about North Dakota are featured on our Book Links page. These links are routinely monitored and updated to provide the most current information available.

www.abdopublishing.com

31

Index